MY FIRST
BOOK OF
ANIMAL
A B C

A

B

C

MY FIRST
BOOK OF
ANIMAL
A B C

Illustrated by Margaret Tarrant

TIGER BOOKS INTERNATIONAL
LONDON

CONTENTS

A a

First in this Animal ABC
Is the Alligator down by the water, you see.
Though Monkey is safe on the letter A,
He'd feel much better if Alligator swam away.

6

B b

B is for the Bears, who can
    walk just like you,
Though you more often see them on
    four legs than two.
There are black bears and white bears,
    and some are born brown;
There's one in the picture who may
    tumble down.

8

C   c

C is for Camel, a beast
   with a hump;
He can move very gently or
   go bumpety-bump.
He lives in the desert, where
   water is rare;
If you saw what he drank at
   one time, you would stare!

D   d

D is for Donkey, a very
    special friend
Who walks on the sandy beach
    from end to end.
Johnny seems to be having a
    wonderful treat,
But I wonder how long he'll
    stay in his seat!

E e

E is for Elephant, big,
    gentle, and wise,
With a very long trunk and
    very small eyes.
He knows what to do when
    little boys tease,
And soon helps them down from
    the tallest of trees.

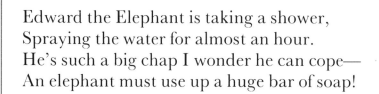

Edward the Elephant is taking a shower,
Spraying the water for almost an hour.
He's such a big chap I wonder he can cope—
An elephant must use up a huge bar of soap!

F f

F is for Fox, an animal sly,
As you surely can guess by
the look in his eye.
I do hope the little birds
perched on the letter
Will soon fly home where they'll
feel much better.

G g

G is for Goat, who can climb very high,
Scrambling up mountains as
   tall as the sky.
Perhaps he is frisky because
   it is spring,
So we can't really blame him for
   dancing the fling.

H   h

H is for Hare, like a soft,
   furry bunny,
But with long pointed ears that
   look very funny.
In a jug Baby Hare is
   trying to hide,
But he's easy to spot
   with his ears left outside.

I i

I is for Ibex, a creature most shy,
Who lives on the mountains
    which soar to the sky.
He is pretty and graceful and
    quick on his toes
And has horns on his head
    wherever he goes.

J j

J is for Jerboa, who has a
    long tail.
If you try to catch him, you
    surely will fail.
He'll fold up his front feet
    and take a long hop,
And down to his underground
    hole he will pop.

K k

K is for Kittens with fur soft as silk;
They love to play, run around,
   and drink lots of milk.
They are useful to have about
   in the house,
And don't they look proud when one
   catches a mouse?

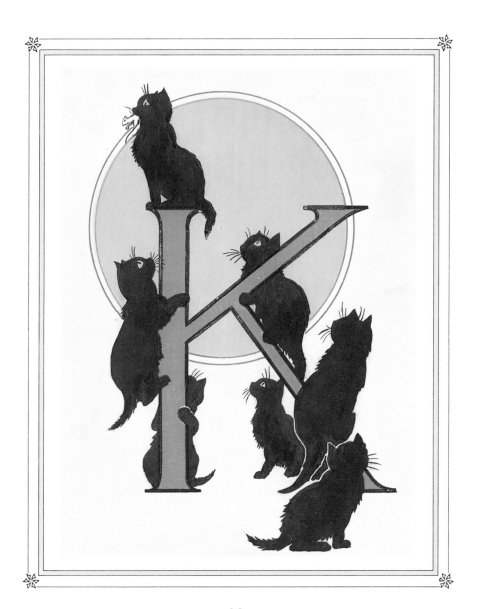

L l

L is for Leopard, well-known
   for his spots;
His eyes in the daytime are
   bright, narrow slots.
When he's prowling around
   in search of his prey,
Wise birds and beasts keep
   out of his way.

M   m

M is for Monkey; as all of you know,
Their tails help them balance
     wherever they go.
One of them has found a mirror
     and hat
And is now dressing up – just
     fancy that . . .

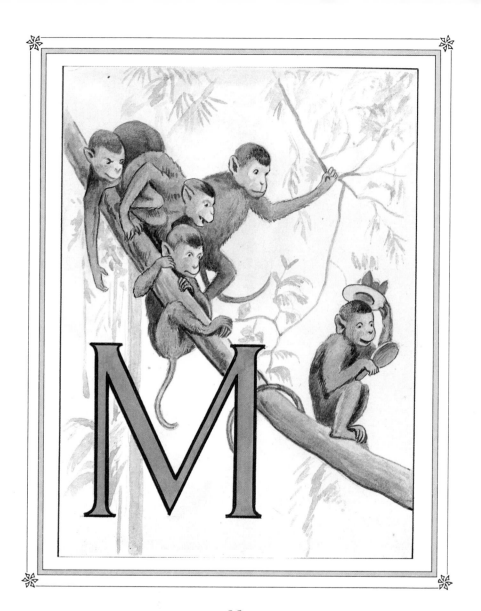

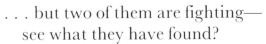

. . . but two of them are fighting—
    see what they have found?
A bag, a comb, a letter that were
    lying on the ground.
The party's not till Saturday in
    the Monkeys' home.
There's time for all of them to dress
    and even use the comb!

N n

N is for the Narwhal, who lives
    among the ice
And is armed with a tusk that doesn't
    look very nice.
When he feels hungry, he swims
    through the sea,
See how he spears a fish
    for his tea!

O o

O is for the Otters, who live
   in our streams
And scare the poor fish from
   their happiest dreams.
They can swim very quickly and
   all like to play;
I do hope you get to meet
   one someday.

P p

P is for the Porcupine
    covered with spines.
Before trying to pet him, you
    should ask if he minds.
When angry or worried he throws
    up his prickles,
But don't ever think that his
    coat just tickles!

Q q

Q is for the Quail, a very
    fine bird,
Whose call in the woods you all
    will have heard.
Look how Johnny the farmer hides
    by the tree,
Counting quail in the grass – one,
    two, and three.

R   r

R is for Reindeer, much loved
   by the Lapps
(And also by Santa Claus,
   the dearest of chaps).
The reindeer is speedy and
   wonderfully strong
And jingles his bells as he
   gallops along.

Each Christmas, the Reindeer pull dear
   Santa's sleigh,
Delivering presents here and far away.
To the roof of each house Santa Claus
   springs,
And the children delight in the toys
   that he brings.

S   s

S is for the Squirrels, who
   live in the trees
And swing from the branches with
   the greatest of ease.
Nuts and acorns they hide
   in the ground,
So they will have food when
   winter comes round.

T t

T is for Tiger with teeth
    sharp as glass.
The stripes on his coat help
    him hide in tall grass.
But now he is hungry, his mouth
    is open wide;
I hope Monkey and his concertina
    don't fall inside!

U u

U is for Umbrella Bird with his
   feathery crest
And a set of plumage that sprouts
   on his breast.
He is a kind of crow and
   a little bit vain,
And I don't think he'd help out much
   in the rain!

V v

V is clearly meant for the Voles,
Water rats who live by the river in holes.
When they want to travel to visit with friends,
They ride on a leaf till their journey ends.

W w

W is for Wolf, a ravenous beast,
Always sniffing around in search
   of a feast.
He is easily scared by a very
   bright light;
Then you can feel safe for the

X x

X is a creature you've not
   met before
And you won't see again, for its
   days are quite o'er.
It roamed over the world when
   people were few;
It's a pity that one wasn't
   saved for the Zoo.

AN E-X-TINCT ANIMAL

Y y

Y is for the Yak who lives
   in Tibet,
Where very few visitors have
   set foot as yet.
He's covered all over with
   long shaggy hair,
Which helps keep him warm when
   there's snow in the air.

Z z

Z is for Zebra with stripes
   white and black
All over his head, his feet and
   his back.
Of course you know also that Z
   stands for Zoo—
A place for all the animals to
   look at me and you!